Knitting Journal

Photo

BELONG TO . . .

NAME . . . .

Index

No.	Pattern Name	For	Date Complete
1			
2			
3			
4			
5			
6			
7			
8			
9			
10			
11			
12			
13			
14			
15			
16			
17			
18			
19			
20			

No.	Pattern Name	For	Date Complete
21			
22			
23			
24			
25			
26			
27			
28			
29			
30			
31			
32			
33			
34			
35			
36			
37			
38			
39			
40			

ISBN-13:978-1985707306
ISBN-10: 1985707306

KNITTING PROJECT

TYPE OF PROJECT : _____

NAME OF PATTERN : _____

FROM : _____

DESIGN : _____

YARN : _____

FIBER CONTENT: _____

COLOR /DYE LOT : _____

WEIGHT: STANDARD _____

WEIGHT NAME : _____

WPI : _____

GAUGE : _____

HOOK SIZE : _____

HOOK TYPE : _____

NOTE : _____

_____

_____

WASHING INSTRUCTIONS : _____

_____

_____

DATE STARTED
GIFT
OCCASION
DATE COMPLETED

FINISH PROJECT PHOTO

YARN LABEL

SMALL SWATCH AND/OR SAMPLE

KNITTING PROJECT

TYPE OF PROJECT : _____

NAME OF PATTERN : _____

FROM : _____

DESIGN : _____

YARN : _____

FIBER CONTENT: _____

COLOR /DYE LOT : _____

WEIGHT: STANDARD _____

WEIGHT NAME : _____

WPI : _____

GAUGE : _____

HOOK SIZE : _____

HOOK TYPE : _____

NOTE : _____

_____

_____

WASHING INSTRUCTIONS : _____

_____

_____

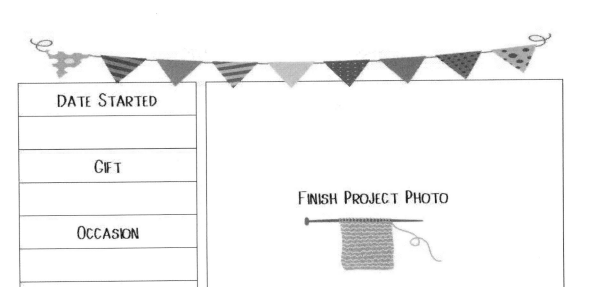

Date Started	
Gift	
Occasion	
Date Completed	

Finish Project Photo

Yarn Label

Small Swatch and/or Sample

KNITTING PROJECT

TYPE OF PROJECT : _____

NAME OF PATTERN : _____

FROM : _____

DESIGN : _____

YARN : _____

FIBER CONTENT: _____

COLOR /DYE LOT : _____

WEIGHT: STANDARD _____

WEIGHT NAME : _____

WPI : _____

GAUGE : _____

HOOK SIZE : _____

HOOK TYPE : _____

NOTE : _____

_____

_____

_____

WASHING INSTRUCTIONS : _____

_____

_____

▷ ▷ ▷ ▷ ▷ ▷ ▷ ▷ ▷ ▷ ▷ ▷ ▷ ▷ ▷ ▷ ▷ ▷ ▷ ☆ ◁

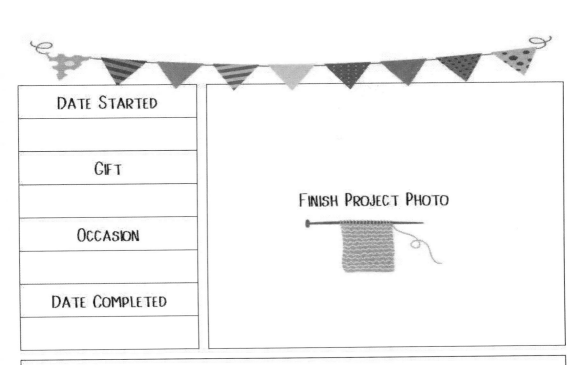

DATE STARTED
GIFT
OCCASION
DATE COMPLETED

FINISH PROJECT PHOTO

YARN LABEL

SMALL SWATCH AND/OR SAMPLE

KNITTING PROJECT

TYPE OF PROJECT : _____

NAME OF PATTERN : _____

FROM : _____

DESIGN : _____

YARN : _____

FIBER CONTENT: _____

COLOR /DYE LOT : _____

WEIGHT: STANDARD _____

WEIGHT NAME : _____

WPI : _____

GAUGE : _____

HOOK SIZE : _____

HOOK TYPE : _____

NOTE : _____

_____

_____

WASHING INSTRUCTIONS : _____

_____

_____

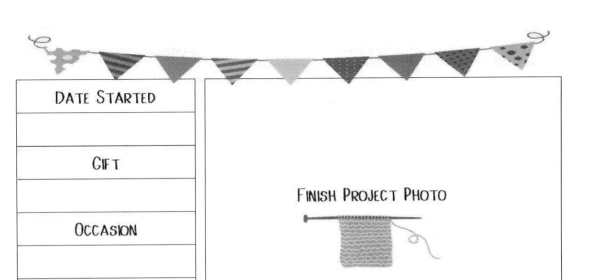

DATE STARTED
GIFT
OCCASION
DATE COMPLETED

FINISH PROJECT PHOTO

YARN LABEL

SMALL SWATCH AND/OR SAMPLE

KNITTING PROJECT

TYPE OF PROJECT : _____

NAME OF PATTERN : _____

FROM : _____

DESIGN : _____

YARN : _____

FIBER CONTENT: _____

COLOR /DYE LOT : _____

WEIGHT: STANDARD _____

WEIGHT NAME : _____

WPI : _____

GAUGE : _____

HOOK SIZE : _____

HOOK TYPE : _____

NOTE : _____

_____

_____

WASHING INSTRUCTIONS : _____

_____

_____

DATE STARTED
GIFT
OCCASION
DATE COMPLETED

FINISH PROJECT PHOTO

YARN LABEL

SMALL SWATCH AND/OR SAMPLE

KNITTING PROJECT

TYPE OF PROJECT : _____

NAME OF PATTERN : _____

FROM : _____

DESIGN : _____

YARN : _____

FIBER CONTENT: _____

COLOR /DYE LOT : _____

WEIGHT: STANDARD _____

WEIGHT NAME : _____

WPI : _____

GAUGE : _____

HOOK SIZE : _____

HOOK TYPE : _____

NOTE : _____

_____

_____

WASHING INSTRUCTIONS : _____

_____

_____

▷▷▷▷▷▷▷▷▷▷▷▷▷▷▷▷▷▷▷ ☆ ◁◁◁◁◁◁◁◁◁◁◁◁◁◁◁◁◁◁◁◁◁◁

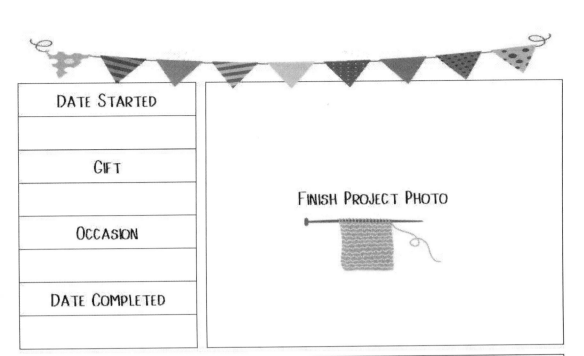

DATE STARTED
GIFT
OCCASION
DATE COMPLETED

FINISH PROJECT PHOTO

YARN LABEL

SMALL SWATCH AND/OR SAMPLE

KNITTING PROJECT

Type of Project : _____

Name of Pattern : _____

From : _____

Design : _____

Yarn : _____

Fiber Content: _____

Color /Dye Lot : _____

Weight: Standard _____

Weight Name : _____

WPI : _____

Gauge : _____

Hook Size : _____

Hook Type : _____

Note : _____

_____

_____

Washing Instructions : _____

_____

_____

▷▷▷▷▷▷▷▷▷▷▷▷▷▷▷▷▷▷▷ ☆ ◁◁◁◁◁◁◁◁◁◁◁◁◁◁◁◁◁◁◁◁◁◁

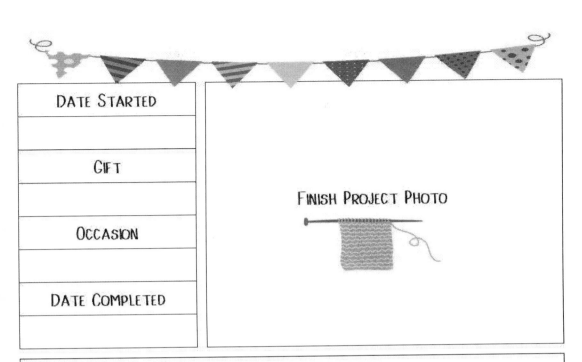

DATE STARTED
GIFT
OCCASION
DATE COMPLETED

FINISH PROJECT PHOTO

YARN LABEL

SMALL SWATCH AND/OR SAMPLE

KNITTING PROJECT

TYPE OF PROJECT : _____

NAME OF PATTERN : _____

FROM : _____

DESIGN : _____

YARN : _____

FIBER CONTENT: _____

COLOR /DYE LOT : _____

WEIGHT: STANDARD _____

WEIGHT NAME : _____

WPI : _____

GAUGE : _____

HOOK SIZE : _____

HOOK TYPE : _____

NOTE : _____

_____

_____

_____

WASHING INSTRUCTIONS : _____

_____

_____

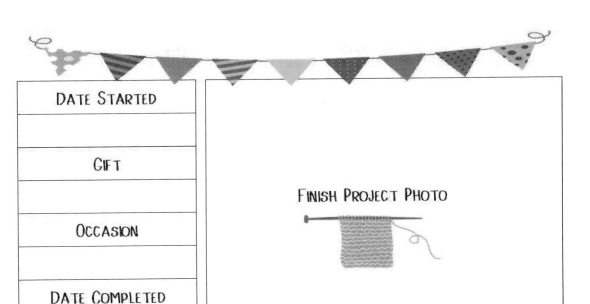

DATE STARTED
GIFT
OCCASION
DATE COMPLETED

FINISH PROJECT PHOTO

YARN LABEL

SMALL SWATCH AND/OR SAMPLE

KNITTING PROJECT

Type of Project : _____

Name of Pattern : _____

From : _____

Design : _____

Yarn : _____

Fiber Content: _____

Color /Dye Lot : _____

Weight: Standard _____

Weight Name : _____

Wpi : _____

Gauge : _____

Hook Size : _____

Hook Type : _____

Note : _____

_____

_____

_____

Washing Instructions : _____

_____

_____

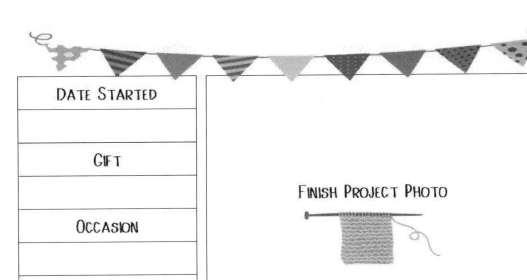

DATE STARTED
GIFT
OCCASION
DATE COMPLETED

FINISH PROJECT PHOTO

YARN LABEL

SMALL SWATCH AND/OR SAMPLE

KNITTING PROJECT

TYPE OF PROJECT : _____

NAME OF PATTERN : _____

FROM : _____

DESIGN : _____

YARN : _____

FIBER CONTENT: _____

COLOR /DYE LOT : _____

WEIGHT: STANDARD _____

WEIGHT NAME : _____

WPI : _____

GAUGE : _____

HOOK SIZE : _____

HOOK TYPE : _____

NOTE : _____

_____

_____

_____

WASHING INSTRUCTIONS : _____

_____

_____

▷ ▷ ▷ ▷ ▷ ▷ ▷ ▷ ▷ ▷ ▷ ▷ ▷ ▷ ▷ ▷ ▷ ☆ ◁

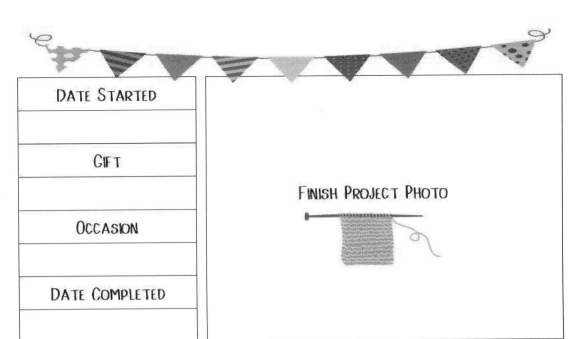

DATE STARTED
GIFT
OCCASION
DATE COMPLETED

FINISH PROJECT PHOTO

YARN LABEL

SMALL SWATCH AND/OR SAMPLE

KNITTING PROJECT

TYPE OF PROJECT : _____

NAME OF PATTERN : _____

FROM : _____

DESIGN : _____

YARN : _____

FIBER CONTENT: _____

COLOR /DYE LOT : _____

WEIGHT: STANDARD _____

WEIGHT NAME : _____

WPI : _____

GAUGE : _____

HOOK SIZE : _____

HOOK TYPE : _____

NOTE : _____

_____

_____

WASHING INSTRUCTIONS : _____

_____

_____

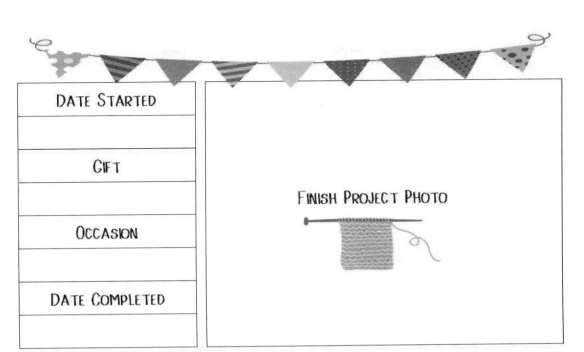

DATE STARTED
GIFT
OCCASION
DATE COMPLETED

FINISH PROJECT PHOTO

YARN LABEL

SMALL SWATCH AND/OR SAMPLE

KNITTING PROJECT

TYPE OF PROJECT : _____

NAME OF PATTERN : _____

FROM : _____

DESIGN : _____

YARN : _____

FIBER CONTENT: _____

COLOR /DYE LOT : _____

WEIGHT: STANDARD _____

WEIGHT NAME : _____

WPI : _____

GAUGE : _____

HOOK SIZE : _____

HOOK TYPE : _____

NOTE : _____

_____

_____

_____

WASHING INSTRUCTIONS : _____

_____

_____

▷ ▷ ▷ ▷ ▷ ▷ ▷ ▷ ▷ ▷ ▷ ▷ ▷ ▷ ▷ ▷ ▷ ☆ ◁

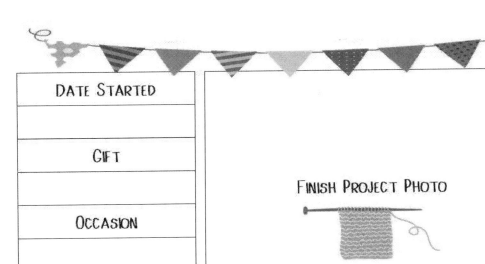

DATE STARTED
GIFT
OCCASION
DATE COMPLETED

FINISH PROJECT PHOTO

YARN LABEL

SMALL SWATCH AND/OR SAMPLE

KNITTING PROJECT

Type of Project : _____

Name of Pattern : _____

From : _____

Design : _____

Yarn : _____

Fiber Content: _____

Color /Dye Lot : _____

Weight: Standard _____

Weight Name : _____

WPI : _____

Gauge : _____

Hook Size : _____

Hook Type : _____

Note : _____

_____

_____

Washing Instructions : _____

_____

_____

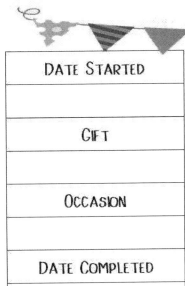

DATE STARTED
GIFT
OCCASION
DATE COMPLETED

FINISH PROJECT PHOTO

YARN LABEL

SMALL SWATCH AND/OR SAMPLE

KNITTING PROJECT

TYPE OF PROJECT : _____

NAME OF PATTERN : _____

FROM : _____

DESIGN : _____

YARN : _____

FIBER CONTENT: _____

COLOR /DYE LOT : _____

WEIGHT: STANDARD _____

WEIGHT NAME : _____

WPI : _____

GAUGE : _____

HOOK SIZE : _____

HOOK TYPE : _____

NOTE : _____

_____

_____

WASHING INSTRUCTIONS : _____

_____

_____

▷ ▷ ▷ ▷ ▷ ▷ ▷ ▷ ▷ ▷ ▷ ▷ ▷ ▷ ▷ ▷ ▷ ☆ ◁ ◁ ◁ ◁ ◁ ◁ ◁ ◁ ◁ ◁ ◁ ◁ ◁ ◁ ◁ ◁ ◁ ◁

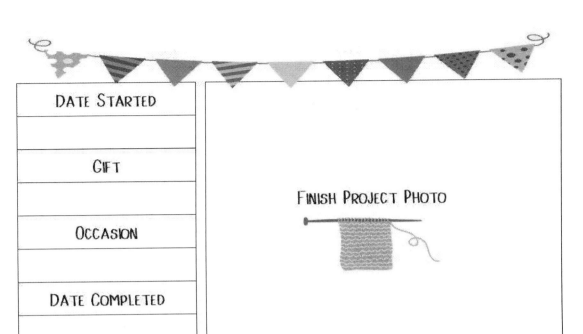

DATE STARTED
GIFT
OCCASION
DATE COMPLETED

FINISH PROJECT PHOTO

YARN LABEL

SMALL SWATCH AND/OR SAMPLE

KNITTING PROJECT

TYPE OF PROJECT : _____

NAME OF PATTERN : _____

FROM : _____

DESIGN : _____

YARN : _____

FIBER CONTENT: _____

COLOR /DYE LOT : _____

WEIGHT: STANDARD _____

WEIGHT NAME : _____

WPI : _____

GAUGE : _____

HOOK SIZE : _____

HOOK TYPE : _____

NOTE : _____

_____

_____

_____

WASHING INSTRUCTIONS : _____

_____

_____

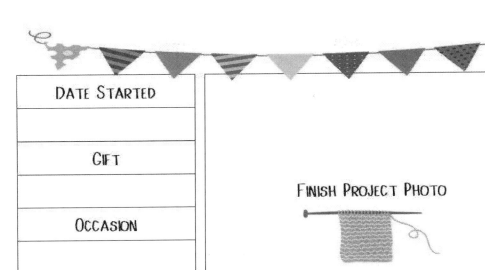

DATE STARTED
GIFT
OCCASION
DATE COMPLETED

FINISH PROJECT PHOTO

YARN LABEL

SMALL SWATCH AND/OR SAMPLE

KNITTING PROJECT

TYPE OF PROJECT : _____

NAME OF PATTERN : _____

FROM : _____

DESIGN : _____

YARN : _____

FIBER CONTENT: _____

COLOR /DYE LOT : _____

WEIGHT: STANDARD _____

WEIGHT NAME : _____

WPI : _____

GAUGE : _____

HOOK SIZE : _____

HOOK TYPE : _____

NOTE : _____

_____

_____

_____

WASHING INSTRUCTIONS : _____

_____

_____

▷▷▷▷▷▷▷▷▷▷▷▷▷▷▷▷▷▷ ☆ ◁◁◁◁◁◁◁◁◁◁◁◁◁◁◁◁◁◁◁◁

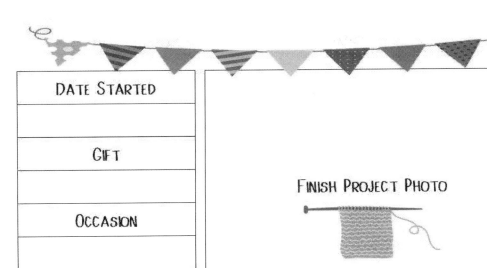

DATE STARTED	
GIFT	
OCCASION	
DATE COMPLETED	

FINISH PROJECT PHOTO

YARN LABEL

SMALL SWATCH AND/OR SAMPLE

KNITTING PROJECT

TYPE OF PROJECT : _____

NAME OF PATTERN : _____

FROM : _____

DESIGN : _____

YARN : _____

FIBER CONTENT: _____

COLOR /DYE LOT : _____

WEIGHT: STANDARD _____

WEIGHT NAME : _____

WPI : _____

GAUGE : _____

HOOK SIZE : _____

HOOK TYPE : _____

NOTE : _____

_____

_____

_____

WASHING INSTRUCTIONS : _____

_____

▷ ▷ ▷ ▷ ▷ ▷ ▷ ▷ ▷ ▷ ▷ ▷ ▷ ▷ ▷ ▷ ▷ ☆ ◁

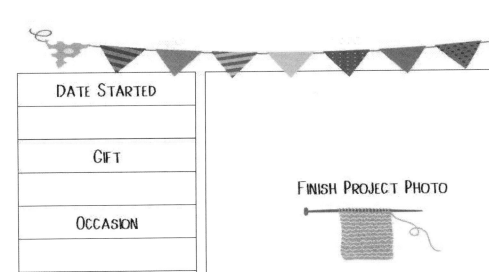

DATE STARTED
GIFT
OCCASION
DATE COMPLETED

FINISH PROJECT PHOTO

YARN LABEL

SMALL SWATCH AND/OR SAMPLE

KNITTING PROJECT

TYPE OF PROJECT : _____

NAME OF PATTERN : _____

FROM : _____

DESIGN : _____

YARN : _____

FIBER CONTENT: _____

COLOR /DYE LOT : _____

WEIGHT: STANDARD _____

WEIGHT NAME : _____

WPI : _____

GAUGE : _____

HOOK SIZE : _____

HOOK TYPE : _____

NOTE : _____

_____

_____

_____

WASHING INSTRUCTIONS : _____

_____

_____

▷▷▷▷▷▷▷▷▷▷▷▷▷▷▷▷▷▷ ☆ ◁◁◁◁◁◁◁◁◁◁◁◁◁◁◁◁◁◁

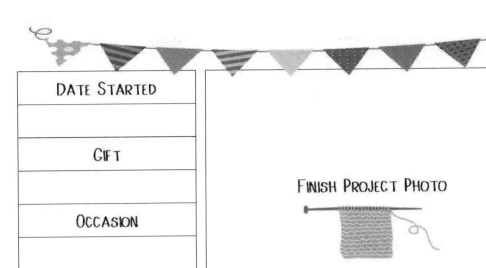

Date Started
Gift
Occasion
Date Completed

Finish Project Photo

Yarn Label

Small Swatch and/or Sample

KNITTING PROJECT

Type of Project : _____

Name of Pattern : _____

From : _____

Design : _____

Yarn : _____

Fiber Content: _____

Color /Dye Lot : _____

Weight: Standard _____

Weight Name : _____

WPI : _____

Gauge : _____

Hook Size : _____

Hook Type : _____

Note : _____

_____

_____

_____

Washing Instructions : _____

_____

_____

▷ ▷ ▷ ▷ ▷ ▷ ▷ ▷ ▷ ▷ ▷ ▷ ▷ ▷ ▷ ▷ ▷ ▷ ☆ ◁

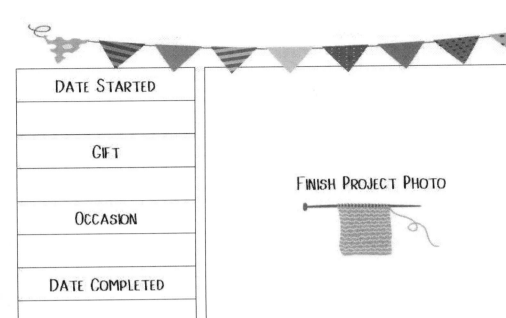

DATE STARTED
GIFT
OCCASION
DATE COMPLETED

FINISH PROJECT PHOTO

YARN LABEL

SMALL SWATCH AND/OR SAMPLE

KNITTING PROJECT

TYPE OF PROJECT : _____

NAME OF PATTERN : _____

FROM : _____

DESIGN : _____

YARN : _____

FIBER CONTENT: _____

COLOR /DYE LOT : _____

WEIGHT: STANDARD _____

WEIGHT NAME : _____

WPI : _____

GAUGE : _____

HOOK SIZE : _____

HOOK TYPE : _____

NOTE : _____

_____

_____

WASHING INSTRUCTIONS : _____

_____

▷ ▷ ▷ ▷ ▷ ▷ ▷ ▷ ▷ ▷ ▷ ▷ ▷ ▷ ▷ ▷ ▷ ▷ ☆ ◁ ◁ ◁ ◁ ◁ ◁ ◁ ◁ ◁ ◁ ◁ ◁ ◁ ◁ ◁ ◁ ◁ ◁

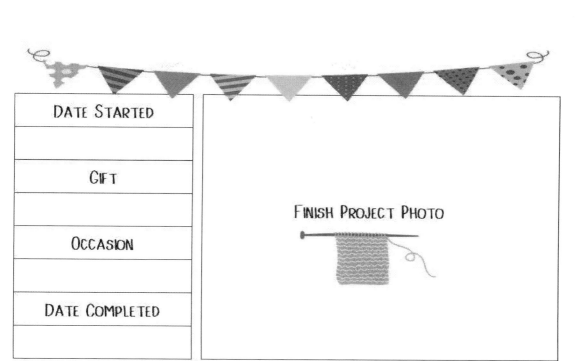

Date Started
Gift
Occasion
Date Completed

Finish Project Photo

Yarn Label

Small Swatch and/or Sample

KNITTING PROJECT

TYPE OF PROJECT : _____

NAME OF PATTERN : _____

FROM : _____

DESIGN : _____

YARN : _____

FIBER CONTENT: _____

COLOR /DYE LOT : _____

WEIGHT: STANDARD _____

WEIGHT NAME : _____

WPI : _____

GAUGE : _____

HOOK SIZE : _____

HOOK TYPE : _____

NOTE : _____

_____

_____

_____

WASHING INSTRUCTIONS : _____

_____

▷▷▷▷▷▷▷▷▷▷▷▷▷▷▷▷▷▷▷ ☆ ◁◁◁◁◁◁◁◁◁◁◁◁◁◁◁◁◁◁◁◁◁◁◁

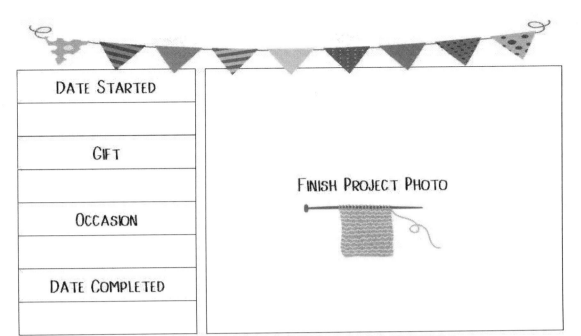

DATE STARTED
GIFT
OCCASION
DATE COMPLETED

FINISH PROJECT PHOTO

YARN LABEL

SMALL SWATCH AND/OR SAMPLE

KNITTING PROJECT

TYPE OF PROJECT : _____

NAME OF PATTERN : _____

FROM : _____

DESIGN : _____

YARN : _____

FIBER CONTENT: _____

COLOR /DYE LOT : _____

WEIGHT: STANDARD _____

WEIGHT NAME : _____

WPI : _____

GAUGE : _____

HOOK SIZE : _____

HOOK TYPE : _____

NOTE : _____

_____

_____

_____

WASHING INSTRUCTIONS : _____

_____

_____

▷ ▷ ▷ ▷ ▷ ▷ ▷ ▷ ▷ ▷ ▷ ▷ ▷ ▷ ▷ ▷ ▷ ☆ ◁ ◁ ◁ ◁ ◁ ◁ ◁ ◁ ◁ ◁ ◁ ◁ ◁ ◁ ◁ ◁ ◁ ◁

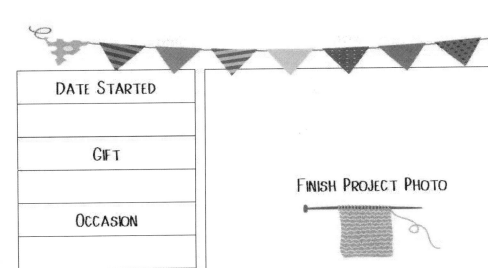

DATE STARTED
GIFT
OCCASION
DATE COMPLETED

FINISH PROJECT PHOTO

YARN LABEL

SMALL SWATCH AND/OR SAMPLE

KNITTING PROJECT

TYPE OF PROJECT : _____

NAME OF PATTERN : _____

FROM : _____

DESIGN : _____

YARN : _____

FIBER CONTENT: _____

COLOR /DYE LOT : _____

WEIGHT: STANDARD _____

WEIGHT NAME : _____

WPI : _____

GAUGE : _____

HOOK SIZE : _____

HOOK TYPE : _____

NOTE : _____

_____

_____

_____

WASHING INSTRUCTIONS : _____

_____

▷▷▷▷▷▷▷▷▷▷▷▷▷▷▷▷▷▷▷▷ ☆ ◁◁◁◁◁◁◁◁◁◁◁◁◁◁◁◁◁◁◁◁◁

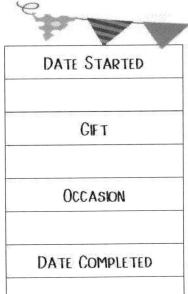

DATE STARTED
GIFT
OCCASION
DATE COMPLETED

FINISH PROJECT PHOTO

YARN LABEL

SMALL SWATCH AND/OR SAMPLE

KNITTING PROJECT

TYPE OF PROJECT : _____

NAME OF PATTERN : _____

FROM : _____

DESIGN : _____

YARN : _____

FIBER CONTENT: _____

COLOR /DYE LOT : _____

WEIGHT: STANDARD _____

WEIGHT NAME : _____

WPI : _____

GAUGE : _____

HOOK SIZE : _____

HOOK TYPE : _____

NOTE : _____

_____

_____

_____

WASHING INSTRUCTIONS : _____

_____

_____

▷ ▷ ▷ ▷ ▷ ▷ ▷ ▷ ▷ ▷ ▷ ▷ ▷ ▷ ▷ ▷ ▷ ▷ ☆ ◁

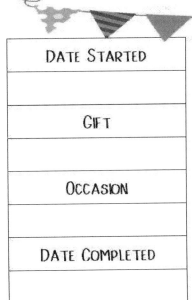

Date Started
Gift
Occasion
Date Completed

Finish Project Photo

Yarn Label

Small Swatch and/or Sample

KNITTING PROJECT

TYPE OF PROJECT : _____

NAME OF PATTERN : _____

FROM : _____

DESIGN : _____

YARN : _____

FIBER CONTENT: _____

COLOR /DYE LOT : _____

WEIGHT: STANDARD _____

WEIGHT NAME : _____

WPI : _____

GAUGE : _____

HOOK SIZE : _____

HOOK TYPE : _____

NOTE : _____

_____

_____

WASHING INSTRUCTIONS : _____

_____

_____

▷ ▷ ▷ ▷ ▷ ▷ ▷ ▷ ▷ ▷ ▷ ▷ ▷ ▷ ▷ ▷ ▷ ▷ ☆ ◁ ◁ ◁ ◁ ◁ ◁ ◁ ◁ ◁ ◁ ◁ ◁ ◁ ◁ ◁ ◁ ◁ ◁

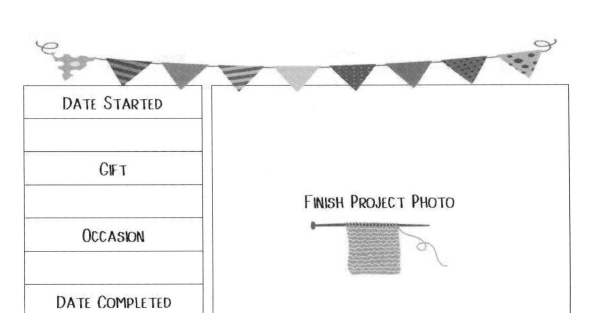

DATE STARTED
GIFT
OCCASION
DATE COMPLETED

FINISH PROJECT PHOTO

YARN LABEL

SMALL SWATCH AND/OR SAMPLE

KNITTING PROJECT

Type of Project : _____

Name of Pattern : _____

From : _____

Design : _____

Yarn : _____

Fiber Content: _____

Color /Dye Lot : _____

Weight: Standard _____

Weight Name : _____

Wpi : _____

Gauge : _____

Hook Size : _____

Hook Type : _____

Note : _____

_____

_____

Washing Instructions : _____

_____

_____

▷ ▷ ▷ ▷ ▷ ▷ ▷ ▷ ▷ ▷ ▷ ▷ ▷ ▷ ▷ ▷ ▷ ▷ ▷ ☆ ◁ ◁ ◁ ◁ ◁ ◁ ◁ ◁ ◁ ◁ ◁ ◁ ◁ ◁ ◁ ◁ ◁ ◁ ◁

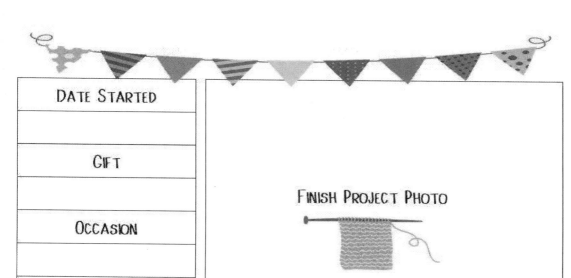

Date Started	
Gift	
Occasion	
Date Completed	

Finish Project Photo

Yarn Label

Small Swatch and/or Sample

KNITTING PROJECT

TYPE OF PROJECT : _____

NAME OF PATTERN : _____

FROM : _____

DESIGN : _____

YARN : _____

FIBER CONTENT: _____

COLOR /DYE LOT : _____

WEIGHT: STANDARD _____

WEIGHT NAME : _____

WPI : _____

GAUGE : _____

HOOK SIZE : _____

HOOK TYPE : _____

NOTE : _____

_____

_____

_____

WASHING INSTRUCTIONS : _____

_____

▷▷▷▷▷▷▷▷▷▷▷▷▷▷▷▷▷▷▷ ☆ ◁◁◁◁◁◁◁◁◁◁◁◁◁◁◁◁◁◁◁◁◁

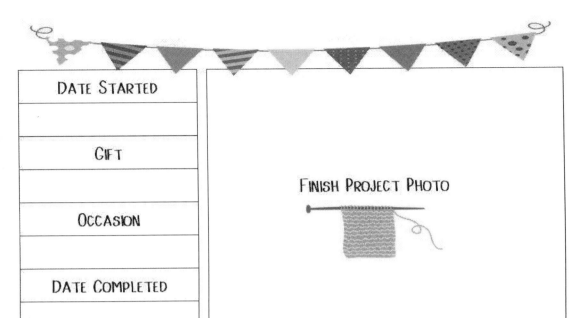

DATE STARTED
GIFT
OCCASION
DATE COMPLETED

FINISH PROJECT PHOTO

YARN LABEL

SMALL SWATCH AND/OR SAMPLE

KNITTING PROJECT

TYPE OF PROJECT : _____

NAME OF PATTERN : _____

FROM : _____

DESIGN : _____

YARN : _____

FIBER CONTENT: _____

COLOR /DYE LOT : _____

WEIGHT: STANDARD _____

WEIGHT NAME : _____

WPI : _____

GAUGE : _____

HOOK SIZE : _____

HOOK TYPE : _____

NOTE : _____

_____

_____

WASHING INSTRUCTIONS : _____

_____

▷ ▷ ▷ ▷ ▷ ▷ ▷ ▷ ▷ ▷ ▷ ▷ ▷ ▷ ▷ ▷ ▷ ☆ ◁ ◁ ◁ ◁ ◁ ◁ ◁ ◁ ◁ ◁ ◁ ◁ ◁ ◁ ◁ ◁ ◁ ◁

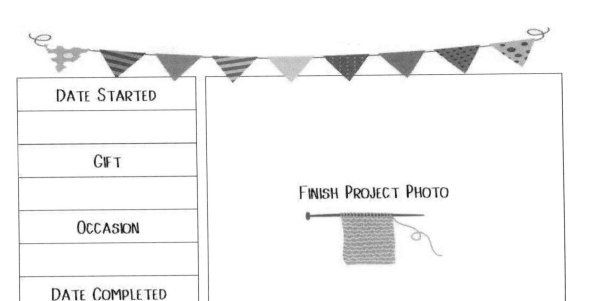

DATE STARTED
GIFT
OCCASION
DATE COMPLETED

FINISH PROJECT PHOTO

YARN LABEL

SMALL SWATCH AND/OR SAMPLE

KNITTING PROJECT

TYPE OF PROJECT : _____

NAME OF PATTERN : _____

FROM : _____

DESIGN : _____

YARN : _____

FIBER CONTENT: _____

COLOR /DYE LOT : _____

WEIGHT: STANDARD _____

WEIGHT NAME : _____

WPI : _____

GAUGE : _____

HOOK SIZE : _____

HOOK TYPE : _____

NOTE : _____

_____

_____

_____

WASHING INSTRUCTIONS : _____

_____

▷ ▷ ▷ ▷ ▷ ▷ ▷ ▷ ▷ ▷ ▷ ▷ ▷ ▷ ▷ ▷ ▷ ▷ ☆ ◁ ◁ ◁ ◁ ◁ ◁ ◁ ◁ ◁ ◁ ◁ ◁ ◁ ◁ ◁ ◁ ◁ ◁

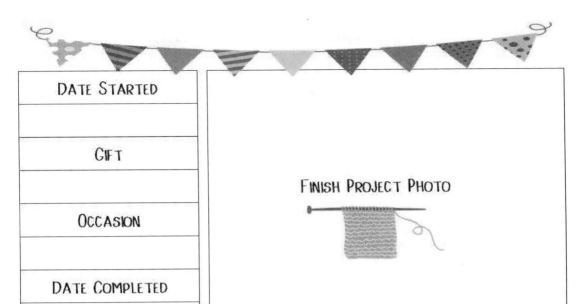

DATE STARTED
GIFT
OCCASION
DATE COMPLETED

FINISH PROJECT PHOTO

YARN LABEL

SMALL SWATCH AND/OR SAMPLE

KNITTING PROJECT

TYPE OF PROJECT : _____

NAME OF PATTERN : _____

FROM : _____

DESIGN : _____

YARN : _____

FIBER CONTENT: _____

COLOR /DYE LOT : _____

WEIGHT: STANDARD _____

WEIGHT NAME : _____

WPI : _____

GAUGE : _____

HOOK SIZE : _____

HOOK TYPE : _____

NOTE : _____

_____

_____

_____

WASHING INSTRUCTIONS : _____

_____

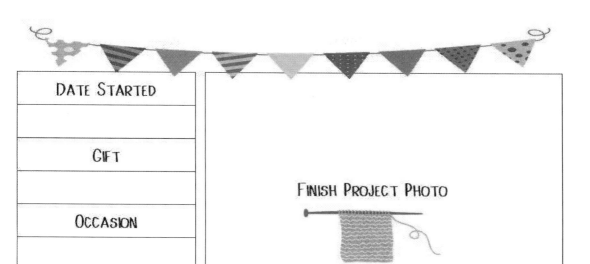

Date Started
Gift
Occasion
Date Completed

Finish Project Photo

Yarn Label

Small Swatch and/or Sample

KNITTING PROJECT

Type of Project : _____

Name of Pattern : _____

From : _____

Design : _____

Yarn : _____

Fiber Content: _____

Color /Dye Lot : _____

Weight: Standard _____

Weight Name : _____

Wpi : _____

Gauge : _____

Hook Size : _____

Hook Type : _____

Note : _____

_____

_____

Washing Instructions : _____

_____

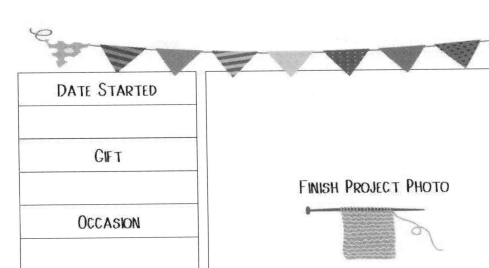

Date Started
Gift
Occasion
Date Completed

Finish Project Photo

Yarn Label

Small Swatch and/or Sample

KNITTING PROJECT

TYPE OF PROJECT : _____

NAME OF PATTERN : _____

FROM : _____

DESIGN : _____

YARN : _____

FIBER CONTENT: _____

COLOR /DYE LOT : _____

WEIGHT: STANDARD _____

WEIGHT NAME : _____

WPI : _____

GAUGE : _____

HOOK SIZE : _____

HOOK TYPE : _____

NOTE : _____

_____

_____

WASHING INSTRUCTIONS : _____

_____

_____

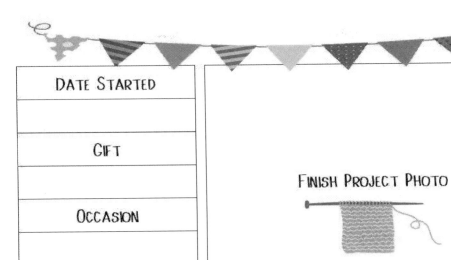

DATE STARTED
GIFT
OCCASION
DATE COMPLETED

FINISH PROJECT PHOTO

YARN LABEL

SMALL SWATCH AND/OR SAMPLE

KNITTING PROJECT

TYPE OF PROJECT : _____

NAME OF PATTERN : _____

FROM : _____

DESIGN : _____

YARN : _____

FIBER CONTENT: _____

COLOR /DYE LOT : _____

WEIGHT: STANDARD _____

WEIGHT NAME : _____

WPI : _____

GAUGE : _____

HOOK SIZE : _____

HOOK TYPE : _____

NOTE : _____

_____

_____

WASHING INSTRUCTIONS : _____

_____

_____

▷▷▷▷▷▷▷▷▷▷▷▷▷▷▷▷▷▷ ☆ ◁◁◁◁◁◁◁◁◁◁◁◁◁◁◁◁◁◁◁◁

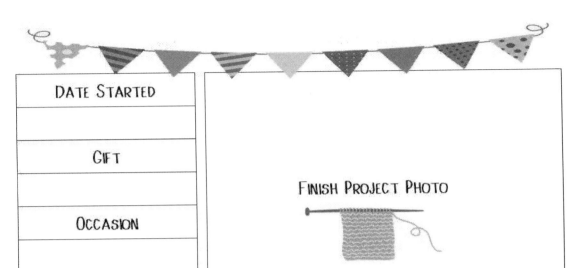

DATE STARTED
GIFT
OCCASION
DATE COMPLETED

FINISH PROJECT PHOTO

YARN LABEL

SMALL SWATCH AND/OR SAMPLE

KNITTING PROJECT

Type of Project : _____

Name of Pattern : _____

From : _____

Design : _____

Yarn : _____

Fiber Content: _____

Color /Dye Lot : _____

Weight: Standard _____

Weight Name : _____

WPI : _____

Gauge : _____

Hook Size : _____

Hook Type : _____

Note : _____

_____

_____

Washing Instructions : _____

_____

_____

▷ ▷ ▷ ▷ ▷ ▷ ▷ ▷ ▷ ▷ ▷ ▷ ▷ ▷ ▷ ▷ ▷ ▷ ▷ ☆ ◁

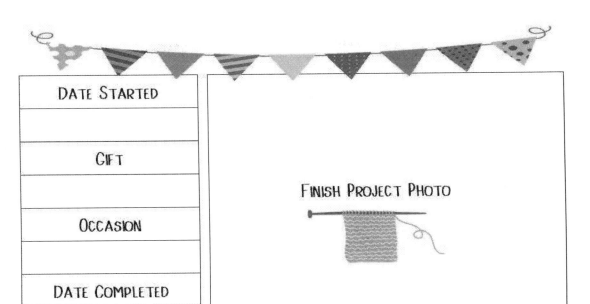

Date Started
Gift
Occasion
Date Completed

Finish Project Photo

Yarn Label

Small Swatch and/or Sample

KNITTING PROJECT

Type of Project : _____

Name of Pattern : _____

From : _____

Design : _____

Yarn : _____

Fiber Content: _____

Color /Dye Lot : _____

Weight: Standard _____

Weight Name : _____

Wpi : _____

Gauge : _____

Hook Size : _____

Hook Type : _____

Note : _____

_____

_____

Washing Instructions : _____

_____

_____

Date Started	
Gift	
Occasion	
Date Completed	

Finish Project Photo

Yarn Label

Small Swatch and/or Sample

KNITTING PROJECT

TYPE OF PROJECT : _____

NAME OF PATTERN : _____

FROM : _____

DESIGN : _____

YARN : _____

FIBER CONTENT: _____

COLOR /DYE LOT : _____

WEIGHT: STANDARD _____

WEIGHT NAME : _____

WPI : _____

GAUGE : _____

HOOK SIZE : _____

HOOK TYPE : _____

NOTE : _____

_____

_____

_____

WASHING INSTRUCTIONS : _____

_____

_____

▷ ☆ ◁

Date Started
Gift
Occasion
Date Completed

Finish Project Photo

Yarn Label

Small Swatch and/or Sample

KNITTING PROJECT

TYPE OF PROJECT : _____

NAME OF PATTERN : _____

FROM : _____

DESIGN : _____

YARN : _____

FIBER CONTENT: _____

COLOR /DYE LOT : _____

WEIGHT: STANDARD _____

WEIGHT NAME : _____

WPI : _____

GAUGE : _____

HOOK SIZE : _____

HOOK TYPE : _____

NOTE : _____

_____

_____

_____

WASHING INSTRUCTIONS : _____

_____

_____

▷ ▷ ▷ ▷ ▷ ▷ ▷ ▷ ▷ ▷ ▷ ▷ ▷ ▷ ▷ ▷ ▷ ▷ ☆ ◁

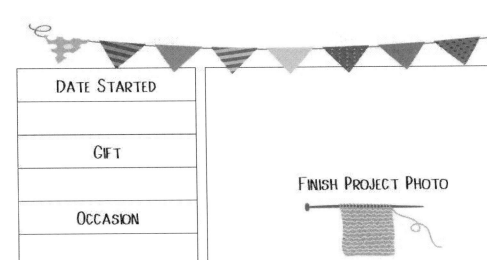

DATE STARTED	
GIFT	
OCCASION	
DATE COMPLETED	

FINISH PROJECT PHOTO

YARN LABEL

SMALL SWATCH AND/OR SAMPLE

KNITTING PROJECT

TYPE OF PROJECT : _____

NAME OF PATTERN : _____

FROM : _____

DESIGN : _____

YARN : _____

FIBER CONTENT: _____

COLOR /DYE LOT : _____

WEIGHT: STANDARD _____

WEIGHT NAME : _____

WPI : _____

GAUGE : _____

HOOK SIZE : _____

HOOK TYPE : _____

NOTE : _____

_____

_____

_____

WASHING INSTRUCTIONS : _____

_____

▷ ▷ ▷ ▷ ▷ ▷ ▷ ▷ ▷ ▷ ▷ ▷ ▷ ▷ ▷ ▷ ▷ ▷ ☆ ◁ ◁ ◁ ◁ ◁ ◁ ◁ ◁ ◁ ◁ ◁ ◁ ◁ ◁ ◁ ◁ ◁ ◁

DATE STARTED	
GIFT	
OCCASION	
DATE COMPLETED	

FINISH PROJECT PHOTO

YARN LABEL

SMALL SWATCH AND/OR SAMPLE

KNITTING PROJECT

TYPE OF PROJECT : _____

NAME OF PATTERN : _____

FROM : _____

DESIGN : _____

YARN : _____

FIBER CONTENT: _____

COLOR /DYE LOT : _____

WEIGHT: STANDARD _____

WEIGHT NAME : _____

WPI : _____

GAUGE : _____

HOOK SIZE : _____

HOOK TYPE : _____

NOTE : _____

_____

_____

_____

WASHING INSTRUCTIONS : _____

_____

_____

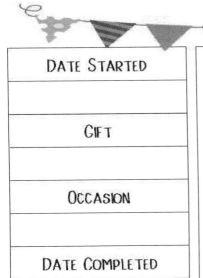

DATE STARTED
GIFT
OCCASION
DATE COMPLETED

FINISH PROJECT PHOTO

YARN LABEL

SMALL SWATCH AND/OR SAMPLE

KNITTING PROJECT

TYPE OF PROJECT : _____

NAME OF PATTERN : _____

FROM : _____

DESIGN : _____

YARN : _____

FIBER CONTENT: _____

COLOR /DYE LOT : _____

WEIGHT: STANDARD _____

WEIGHT NAME : _____

WPI : _____

GAUGE : _____

HOOK SIZE : _____

HOOK TYPE : _____

NOTE : _____

_____

_____

_____

WASHING INSTRUCTIONS : _____

_____

_____

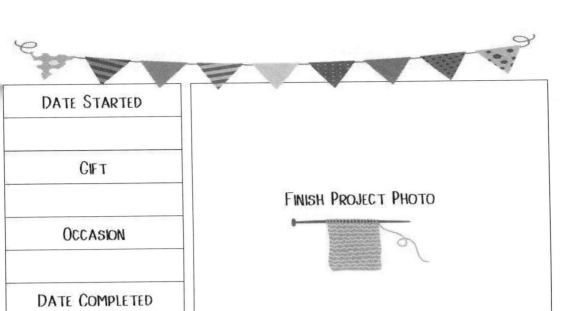

DATE STARTED
GIFT
OCCASION
DATE COMPLETED

FINISH PROJECT PHOTO

YARN LABEL

SMALL SWATCH AND/OR SAMPLE

 N TES

 NTES

 NTES

 NTES

 NTES

 N**O**TES

 NTES

 NTES

 NTES

 NTES

 NTES

N TES

 N TES

 NTES

 NTES

 NTES

 NTES

 NTES

 NTES

Made in the USA
Middletown, DE
18 November 2021

52803323R00057